For the love of all that is cute,
silly, and Furbish, the furby
fan community presents...

# Big Fun!
## A Furby Fanzine

(We've all worked hard on this,
and we hope you enjoy looking at it!)

**Cover illustration by Artichuka on Tumblr
March 2017**

A. Moore

"The History of Furby"

# THE HISTORY OF FURBY
## A. MOORE

IN FEBRUARY OF 1997, DAVE HAMPTON WENT TO THE AMERICAN INTERNATIONAL TOY FAIR, WHERE HE SAW THE TAMAGOTCHI FOR THE FIRST TIME.

HE WASN'T TO IMPRESSED BY IT, AND HAS SAID THAT HE FOUND IT TO BE TOO STERILE AND "FLAT." SOON AFTER, HE STARTED DESIGNING THE CHILDREN'S TOY THE TAMAGOTCHI INSPIRED: THE FURBY.

IT TOOK HAMPTON AND PARTNER CALEB CHUNG NINE MONTHS TO CREATE THE FIRST FURBY PROTOTYPE, AND AFTER THEY INVITED FELLOW TOY AND GAME INVENTOR RICHARD C. LEVY TO HELP SELL IT, LEVY BROUGHT FURBY TO TIGER ELECTRONICS, A TOY COMPANY WHICH HAD JUST BEEN BOUGHT BY HASBRO IN JUNE OF 1998.

WHEN THE FIRST FURBY PROTOTYPE WAS SHOWN TO ALAN G. HASSENFELD, CHAIRMAN OF TIGER, THERE WERE APPARENTLY SOME PROBLEMS GETTING IT TO START, AS THE HALOGEN LIGHT BULBS IN THE ROOM WERE INTERFERING WITH THE SIGNALS BEING SENT ALONG A WIRE BETWEEN THE FURBY AND THE CONCEALED BLACK EMULATOR BOX THAT CONTAINED ITS MACHINERY. TIN FOIL WAS WRAPPED AROUND THE WIRE TO SHIELD IT FROM THE RADIATION, AND AFTER THE FURBY DID TURN ON AND HASSENFELD SAW IT WORKING, HE REPORTED TO ROGER SHIFFMAN, THE PRESIDENT OF TIGER, THAT IT WAS THE COOLEST THING HE'D SEEN IN 25 YEARS IN THE BUSINESS.

NOT LONG AFTER, SHIFFMAN BOUGHT THE RIGHTS TO THE FURBY, AND PRODUCTION BEGAN WITH THE GOAL OF MAKING IT AVAILABLE IN TIME FOR CHRISTMAS OF 1998. SHIFFMAN ACKNOWLEDGED THE RISK OF RUSHING PRODUCTION, BUT SAID IT WAS "TOO EXCITING NOT TO TRY."

FURBIES BEGAN FLYING OFF THE SHELVES AS SOON AS THEY WERE RELEASED IN STORES ON OCTOBER 2ND, 1998. SOME STORES WERE SO WORRIED ABOUT THE FRENZY THAT THEY WOULDN'T EVEN LET BUYERS GET THEM DIRECTLY FROM

A. Moore

"The History of Furby" (continued)

THE SHELF - ANYONE WHO WANTED TO PURCHASE A FURBY HAD TO GET A TICKET AND GIVE THAT TO A STORE ASSOCIATE, WHO WOULD THEN GIVE YOU THE FURBY. IT WAS THE YEAR'S HOTTEST TOY.

IN DECEMBER THOUGH, A RUMOR OF A POTENTIAL LAWSUIT BY WARNER BROS. TOOK OFF, AS THE SIMILARITIES BETWEEN FURBIES AND MOGWAI (THE CREATURES THAT MORPHED INTO GREMLINS IN THE MOVIE BY THE SAME NAME) WERE NOT LOST ON THEM OR ANYONE ELSE.

ANOTHER RUMOR APPEARED IMMEDIATELY AFTER THAT A SEVEN-FIGURE SETTLEMENT HAD TAKEN PLACE. THE RUMORS WERE DISPUTED BY WARNER BROS. SPOKESPERSON BARBARA BROGLIATTO, WHO SAID, "THERE WAS NOT A LAWSUIT AND THERE'S NO SETTLEMENT. WE HAVE A GOOD WORKING RELATIONSHIP WITH HASBRO."

WARNER BROS. EVEN PARTNERED WITH TIGER TO BRING THE GIZMO FURBY FRIEND TO CONSUMERS, AND THOSE AND OTHER FURBIES CONTINUED TO ENJOY THE SAME POPULARITY WELL INTO THE NEXT YEAR. IN 1999 TIGER RELEASED FURBY BABIES, WHICH WERE SMALLER FURBIES WITH DIFFERENT VOICES AND EASTER EGGS, AND FURBY BUDDIES, WHICH WERE ALSO EXTREMELY POPULAR IN 1999 AND 2000 THEY PARTNERED WITH MCDONALD'S TO GIVE AWAY LITTLE FURBY FIGURES AND KEYCHAINS, RESPECTIVELY, AND EVEN THOSE WERE CONSIDERED COLLECTIBLE.

THE HYPE COULD ONLY LAST FOR SO LONG THOUGH, BECAUSE TIGER STARTED RELEASING SO MANY DIFFERENT VARIATIONS OF FURBY AND FURBY BABIES THAT THE MARKET BECAME OVERSATURATED AND SALES STARTED DWINDLING. THE COMPANY STOPPED SELLING FURBIES IN 2000, AND INSTEAD STARTED FOCUSING ON A FURBY OFFSHOOT CALLED SHELBY, WHICH WAS RELEASED IN 2001. IN 2002, THOSE TOO WERE RETIRED FROM THE TIGER LINE.

SO WHAT BECAME OF TIGER'S FURBY? TODAY THEY ARE STILL BOUGHT AND SOLD ON AUCTION SITES, RELICS OF A BYGONE ERA WITH A FANBASE THAT WILL NOT LET GO OF THEM.

Luna Lehmann

"May-May Selfie!!"

Froth Essex

"Status Symbol"

Alex C.

"Furby Circus"

Ash Tetreau

"FURBY DREAMING"

Dara (drippingbat.tumblr.com)

"Potion Master"

KS Collins

"Wah!"

guanojuice@tumblr

Prince of Puns

"Bouncin' Baby Blue"

Player_056

"Furby Dreams"

Bart Anderson

"My Furby"

Bryce Lynn

"Onion Boy"

A. Moore

"Flying South for the Winter"

Flying south for the winter...

Aibo7m3

"Spring"

Wolfgang Zoe

"Pumpkin Patch"

Alex C.

"Coolin'"

Manufactured by Amazon.ca
Acheson, AB

11955320R00021